"Tea for the Wicked"
© 2024 by Serena Morrigan

All rights reserved. No part of this publication may be reproduced, distributed, or transmitted in any form or by any means, including photocopying, recording, or other electronic or mechanical methods, without the prior written permission of the publisher, except in the case of brief quotations embodied in critical reviews and certain other non-commercial uses permitted by copyright law. For permission requests, write to the publisher, addressed "Attention: Permissions Coordinator," at the e-mail address below.

Serena.Morrigan@gmail.com
Instagram: @Serena.Morrigan

ISBN (paperback): 978-3-9823098-2-8
ISBN (e-book): 978-3-9823098-3-5

Edited by Brooke Goodwin
Cover & Interior by Dot Ink Agency

Serena Morrigan
c/o AutorenServices.de
Birkenallee 24
D-36037 Fulda

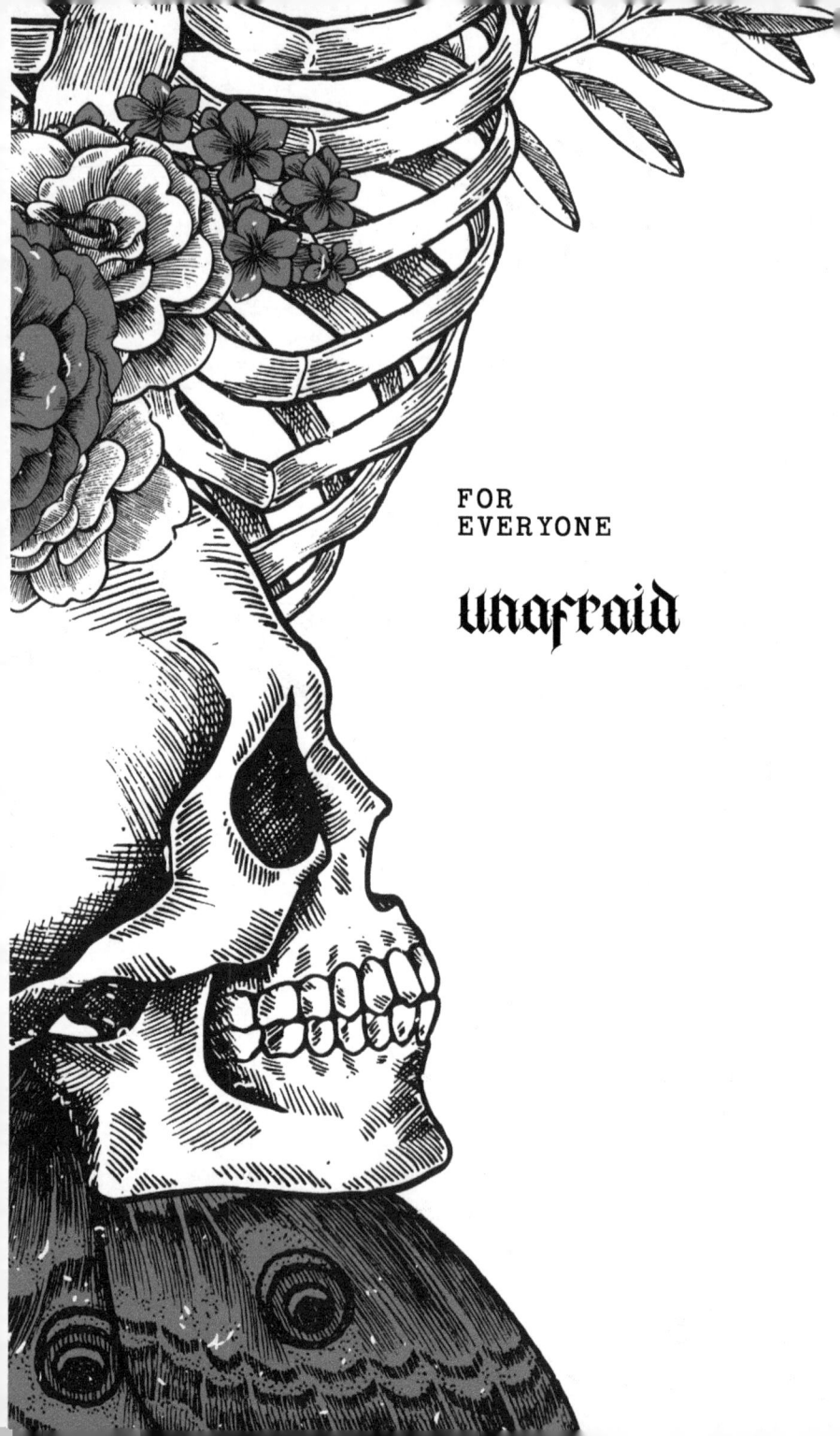

other books

A SONG FOR EVERY SCAR (2021)

intro

**SOMEWHERE IT'S
ALWAYS TIME
FOR TEA**

Welcome to my little witches' circle where only the most intrepid meet. These pages are your ticket to a gruesome world full of dark magic and macabre tales that will make your blood run cold.

I hope you'll enjoy the madness hiding in every poem, the sublimity between each line like syrupy goo. A twisted carnival for the brave only, so continue at your own risk! In this fantastical world of horror, we're all mad here.

Yours,
Serena Morrigan

inspiration

"NO GREAT MIND HAS EVER EXISTED WITHOUT A TOUCH OF MADNESS."

- ARISTOTLE

trigger warnings

DEATH
MURDER
VIOLENCE
GORE
SUICIDE

carnival carnage
1 5 - 3 3

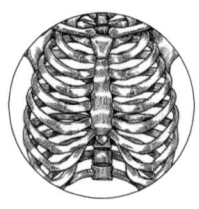

gothic grotesque
3 5 - 5 4

asylum anthologies
5 7 - 7 2

macabre melancholy
75 - 92

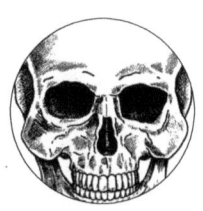

graveyard grimoire
95 - 111

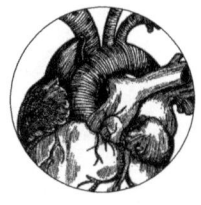

haunted hearts
113 - 128

carnival carnage

FIRST COURSE

There's something underneath this skin
Holding me prisoner in my own mind;
The way I've always known it and
THERE'S NO WAY OUT –
How to get out of this labyrinth?
Escalation – my middle name,
Pushing myself over the edge
Just to feel something, *anything*;
Welcome to the freak show
I said, WELCOME TO THE FREAK SHOW!
Oh, the fun we're going to have –
The haunted house is filled with screams
Ready to lash out at you at any moment;
You've got to be fearless if you want to
Deal with the wicked ones
Screaming your name with bruised lungs;
I am the Wicked, burning at the stakes,
Screaming curses at the living

I'm so long dead, was I ever alive?

Come one! Come all!
To this most bizarre show!

And don't mind the clown, he's always been weird
With his terrible grin, gosh, those frightful teeth;
He's just sitting there on a swing high up in the air,
But please, dear friends, enjoy yourselves –
As the first act of the night enters the circus ring:
Horridini, the greatest magician of our time –
You won't believe your eyes when he manifests
Your grandmother who's been ten years dead,
Strapping her to a table to cut her in two –
Oh, how the blood splatters, like confetti!
What a show! What a show! What a massacre!
We hope you'll grace us with your presence
The next time, it will be your torso atwain

Meet the mime they call Monsieur –
Entertaining young and old alike;
With a big smile on his pale face –
Watch as it slowly gives way to panic;
Don't you see the distress in his eyes?
While hands trace an invisible wall;
He's a voiceless creature, poor soul,
A prisoner of his mind, he can't escape;
For it is dignity he cannot express
With his skinny, white-gloved hands
And thus ends the show with a BANG!
His striped shirt blood-stained,
Gunshot residue on his gloves

Underneath the circus tent,
A rope spun tightly from wall to wall –
Thin as a hair, made of sharpened steel –
The funambulist keeps her balance
As she slowly crosses your spinal cord
With a smile and a scythe in hand

Onlookers watch the artists in the ring
"There's blood in the arena!" they sing
As the intoxicated acrobat sways
On the trapeze, back and forth,
While mechanical monkeys laugh
And bang their cymbals boisterously –
The whole vaudevillage at play –
As the ringmaster shouts:
"Welcome to the Circus Macabre!"
Knives piercing nothing but the heart
"There's blood in the arena!" they sing

With their hearts sinking they watch
Horses, once tame and timid, run wild,
Leaving the audience gasping before
Roars lift up into the air, a stampede of sound;
Every adult, all the children, petrified –
They simply cannot believe their eyes
As daggers fly across the rows of spectators

Wrinkled, with amber-coloured eyes,
Beautifully dressed in delicate fabrics,
Mary performs her tricks as she's told,
While painful memories rest within

The ringmaster's voice still echoing
In her enormous yet leaf-like ears,
Reminding her of all her past mistakes,
As the whip lashes against her trunk

The shocked audience watches in horror –
Dreadful scenes unfolding in the spotlight,
As the massive elephant attacks the host
With ivory tusks & heavy limbs she strikes

Horrified visitors running for their lives,
Leaving the ringmaster in crimson dirt,
While Mary continues her killing spree
Until all her tormentors have been slain

She already knew what was to come –
Hunted down she died the day after,
Hanged by villagers in the marketplace,
Mary's revenge echoing through the ages

Minnie's Soliloquy:

These daggers I will poison carefully,
For it will be your last show tonight;
Try swallowing these, my dear Ethel –
Your true colours about to be revealed!

Ethel's Soliloquy:

I laced the lamp oil with cyanide,
It will leave a deadly taste;
Try breathing tonight, Minnie –
The fire in your eyes extinguished!

***

CARNIVAL CARNAGE

And what a show it was, indeed!
When the sword swallower
Performed her trick that night
And the fire breather took a sip,
Unaware of death's presence in the ring,
As both collapsed, eyes locked –
Dagger still stuck in Ethel's throat,
Minnie's final breath a tragedy –
Setting the circus tent on fire;
No escape for the wicked –
No escape for the innocent

A crooked melody in the distance –
Electric lights flickering erratically –
This is Dreamland
Where there's so much more to see

The carousel rusted from acidic rain,
Creaking to the maniacal laughter
Of oblivious visitors watching
The terribly performed disaster

A ferris wheel spinning rather slowly,
Overlooking the colossal pavilion –
Where gaudy actors rest and drink –
Watching the inebriated vaudevillians

The wooden roller coaster, in flames –
Once a wonderland, now an abandoned site
Where the adventurous crowd passed the time;
Destroyed by fire one fateful night

Let me show you a place you'll love
A cabinet of mirrors and of wax
Where you cannot tell what's real.
　　　　　　　　　　What's not?
Here, feel their skin? Silky smooth!
No, he wasn't blinking, it's all in your mind –
You've seen too many horror movies;
This is a respectable business, I dare say,
Just as Madame had pictured it to be;
Let me look at your pretty face –
You'd make a wonderful model, my child;
Just stand right there and DON'T MOVE!
While I get my pot of scorching-hot wax

AFTER DYLAN THOMAS

Do not go gentle into that good night,
For you never know what might lurk
Inside the corners of the darkest mind,
Hiding away from an innocent light

Grisly thoughts pressed against the skull
Scream louder than your desperate pleas
To stop the blazing madness in its tracks
And to return to something once magical

Do not go gentle into that good night
Where monsters feast & demons play
Inside the corners of the darkest mind,
They're always ready for another fight

MY CHILDHOOD HOME · MY CHILDHOOD HOME · MY CHILDHOOD HOME · MY CHILDHOOD HOME

Give me your hand and let me guide you
Through the house that was my childhood home;
It has been years since I was last here,
But still everything feels so familiar;
Even though the wallpaper is cracked & peeled
And the windows have been shattered,
The furniture is still where it used to be –
Trust me, I know my way around here –
Now take this candle and follow me
To the last room down the dim hallway
Where I spent so many hours playing with dolls;
Look, they're still there! Their clothes are ragged,
But their porcelain faces are still beautiful
– Wait, what did you say?
      No, their eyes can't move on their own,
   You must be imagining things;
          Look, how lovely they are!
               This is not a haunted house, darling –

This is a haunted home.

It's dark outside,
All the lights are out,
I'm all alone in my bed
Trying to get some sleep,
But what's that sound?
Someone's laughing
Or is someone crying?
Where does it come from?
That voice in my room –
I thought I was alone;
Now the closet door's creaking
And gloved fingers are reaching
For the doorknob most delicately,
Until a wide grin, massive & cruel,
Emerges from within my closet –
In terror, I scream!

But the creature I see
Comes closer nevertheless;
This is my end, I see it so clear,
In the papers they will state:

*"She died with a terrible
Smile on her face
And a plastic flower
Stuck in her chest"*

Enter these dark halls, don't be afraid –
There's nothing scarier than
The *happiness* in their eyes;
Watch as the Black drips down these walls,
Blending with a thick pool of crimson
Onto these marble floors, cold as death;
You will find her crouching like a beast
In a pile of tulle on her skeletal throne,
Despising every ray of light;
She is dressed in cataclysmic demise,
She built a castle of infinite night
And banned every hint of sanity;
She's the Queen of the Macabre –
Dipping the world in madness;
She knows her way among the dead,
Singing an eerie lullaby for all the lost souls
Afraid of the ordinary & mundane;
This Palace of Paranoia is a refuge
For all the demons in your head

Welcome to the Masquerade
Enter at your free will, I implore you;
Behind the curtain adorned with bats,
The monster ball is already in full swing;
Moths attracted to the neon lights
Dance under the cobwebbed ceiling;
You'll have the time of your life
As you waltz with the fiercely dead –
Limbs strewn across the ballroom

The irresistible allure of
A monster masquerade

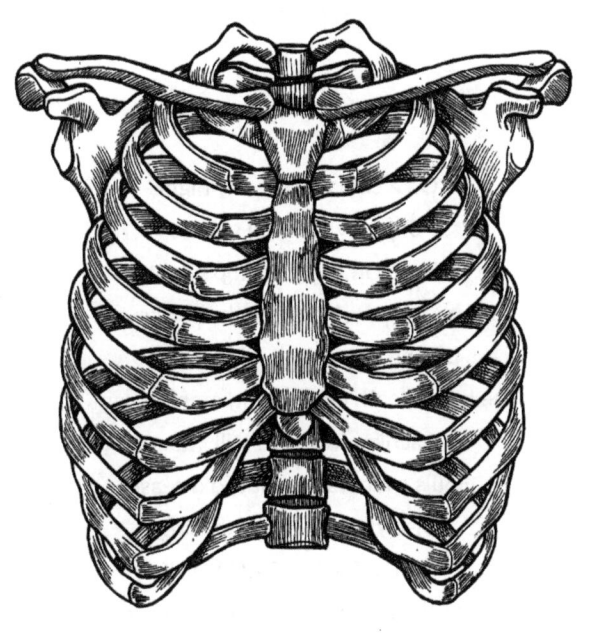

gothic grotesque

SECOND COURSE

On a cold and stormy night,
Slippery cobbled streets
Glisten in the gas lamp's light;
The fog pouring through the alleys
Like an army of ghosts forlorn –
The black death omniscient, omnipresent –
Reaching for lungs still intact;
Souls evaporating, putrid disease;
Distorted voices screaming:
"WE CANNOT SAVE YOU!"
As the mourner's desperate wails
Wax and wane with the moon
And the flies and worms multiply,
Gorging on a feast of rotten flesh;
No, we cannot save you,
But some will survive this chaos,
Wiping the black from the canvas
To rebuild what has been lost

GOTHIC GROTESQUE

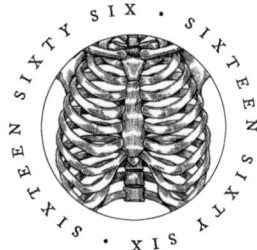

As if the Plague hadn't been enough,
I sit and watch my life burn –
The narrow streets & crooked alleys
Quickly fill with raging panic;
It should have been a beautiful Sunday,
Now futile prayers & soot rise to the sky;
And no fire hook or river may stop
The unconsecrated cremation of life –
It's a firestorm, and Lord only knows
If I'll make it out of this Hell alive

The year was 1666 when the Devil
Roamed through the City of London

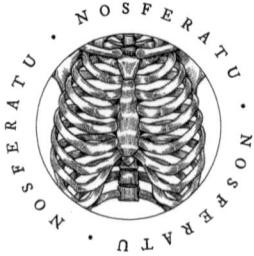

The sun is setting as I rise
From the ashes, sacred earth
And these halls come back to life,
As the candles light themselves;
My oblivious guest is fast asleep –
I laced his wine with bromide –
Tonight my brides and I will feast,
As this young man's life subsides

GOTHIC GROTESQUE

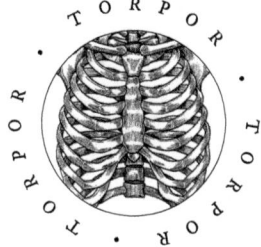

Is there nothing more to say?
No words left to twist and bend;
I carved poetry out of my bones
Until there was nothing left of me;
Promise me this is not the end,
That I am merely æstivating;
Inspiration patiently waiting
In the Carpathian Mountains

When I can't sleep at night
I look out my Venetian window
Overlooking the stormy sea;
Watching the waves is calming,
But tonight I have a welcome guest –
I've befriended a jet-black bat
Keeping me company every other night,
Letting me stroke its tiny head –
A mesmerising creature with wings,
Lulling me back to sleep...

But why oh why, every morning,
Do I wake up so weak & pallid?
A mystery yet to be solved;
The maritime breeze seems useless
And these two little needle pricks
From a scarf fastened too tight
From when I – oh, please don't tell mother! –
When I walked about at night
Unconscious; saved by my friend;
These marks, they haven't healed...

Covered in white linen she lies –
Beautiful, yet pale like a ghost –
An illness eventually took its toll;
Her last breath a kiss on my lips

I buried her on a Sunday morn
In the family vault, she will reside –
A place inhabited much too soon;
Here, I pray, she'll rest in peace

Three days went by in torturous grief,
When finally I regained my strength
To visit her burial site again –
So as to weep my final goodbyes

Only then I saw what froze my blood
And ultimately tore my heart in two –
The vault door ajar; my love – snatched!
But, dear Lord, what I saw within!

GOTHIC GROTESQUE

No grave robbers had dared to touch
My bride's bones laid so beautifully,
But, oh, the sight was just too cruel!
As she stared right into my eyes...

Good heavens! Oh, what terrible fate!
My poor love had been buried alive!
For two days, she'd tried to free herself,
But only got so far before she succumbed

It's been a year since I last saw her face,
Her eyes are still haunting me at night
And I will never forget the horror I felt
When I saw her frightened hazel eyes

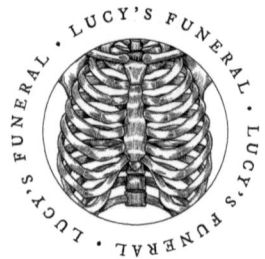

I close this coffin
With a smile on my face;
My work here is done,
As I leave the sacred vault;
Her skin's iridescent glow
And sharp canine teeth –
A most unnatural state,
Unlike the Creator's intent,
Now a thing of the past;
Her mortal beauty
Has been restored tonight –

GOTHIC GROTESQUE

Beheaded by her lover's hand
And a wooden stake in
The centre of her undying heart –
A scream escapes her lungs –
She will rest in peace
Among these alliaceous flowers;
The Devil will not find
His way back into this grave

Yours sincerely,
𝔙𝔞𝔫 ℌ𝔢𝔩𝔰𝔦𝔫𝔤

There's something familiar about this creature
Made up of human remains exhumed at night,
Stitched together & revived –
The secret of life revealed –
A concept not too far off from reality,
If you think about it...

Just like my heart, this undying, crazy thing –
It's made up of pieces of strangers' hearts,
Stitched together & revived –
The secret of love revealed –
This mosaic of a heart still beats,
Despite the suffering...

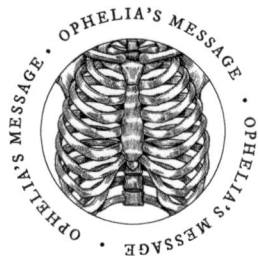

From beyond the grave,
In linen river-soaked –
She inhales fatality
And exhales tragedy

The water lily floats,
Carelessly trimmed,
Caressing pale limbs,
As she fades away

On a rainy night in Victorian London,
The group of spiritualists assemble;
Around the table, they take their seats –
The table cloth – cascades of crimson satin –
Illuminated by soft candlelight

Holding hands, they murmur invocations
To summon the spirits of ancestors,
To hear their voices one last time
And ask for guidance & forgiveness;
A sudden puff blows out the candlelight

GOTHIC GROTESQUE

Aquiver, the spiritualists sing & sway,
Mindless, they've ignored the signs,
As evil spirits manifest in the candles' smoke –
Ready to punish the ones guilty of living,
Regardless of the candlelight

The attendees shocked & paralysed,
While the most gruesome scene unfolds:
A dagger for every heart alive –
They're damned to roam the spirit realm,
Haunted by soft candlelight

The ocean gently calls her name at night,
When dark waves crash against the shore
And sirens sing their songs of solitude –
She will follow the voices in her head,
Pulling her closer to the starlit coast;
She's not afraid of what's to come –
The depths of these boisterous waters,
About to swallow her whole, recklessly;
She doesn't mind the spins & whirls –
You'll find her at the bottom of the ocean
Where she will gather her strength again,
For she was born with mermaid lungs
To face the tempest at land and sea

GOTHIC GROTESQUE

As I enter the anatomical theatre
I make my way through the skeletons;
I'll be an attentive observer tonight
When my professor Dr. Seward arrives
To dissect another body for science's sake –
So that we, the students, may be taught
About the anatomy of the insane;
I hope it will not end up in goo again;
Another corpse, another morbid autopsy,
But something is fairly different tonight –
Electricity's crackling, metal clanging,
And a loud scream roars through the rows:
"I AM ALIVE," the resurrected mumbles,
Looking about, weak and confused,
It has been done, oh, wonders of science!
In marvellous horror I observe the scene,
While "Memento Mori" painted on the walls
Reminds us of a now obsolete belief,
Since immortality has been achieved!

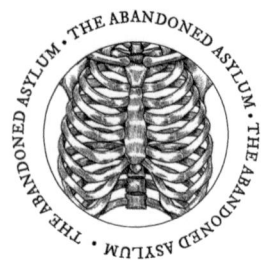

The Abandoned Asylum

Empty hallways, ravaged dormitories,
Desperate pleas scribbled on the walls;
A place, abandoned by the living –
Once a last resort for the broken girl,
Interrupted by disaster, desolate;

Medication scattered on the floor,
A ragged doll propped up against
The remnants of the padded cell –
Haunting eyes and an evil smirk
Grace her distraught porcelain face

We better leave, it's not safe here;
The ghosts of a thousand lost souls
Remain hidden in the cracks –
I sense their presence, don't you?
Let's leave and never come back

asylum anthologies

THIRD COURSE

More tea for the Wicked.

Oh, how I love the madness in their eyes –

For I am crazy, too

Turning the world upside down,
My fingers grasping air

More cake for the Damned.

Baked goods from the hellfire

To sustain the erratic mind

As soon as twilight fades and darkness unfolds –
You'll find me in a corner, writing time away
About all the monsters & ghosts chasing me;
They've been with me on this journey for so long;
When the sun sets they come out to play,
With their distorted smiles & ghoulish minds;
I hope you're not afraid of the dark, dear –
Because this is the world I grew up in,
I will stay here for a while longer
And so will they...

These bodies at my feet
Are identities I've shed –
Like an ordinary caterpillar
Sheds its skin before
Becoming a beautiful butterfly;
But I became a moth –
Creature of the night –
I turned towards the light,
Burned by the fire,
This part of me died, too;
And so I roam the streets
Looking for something new
To imitate & make my own –
As a master of disguise –
I've forgotten who I really am

Let this ink pour like rain
Onto this paper I call my skin;
Wash away this loneliness
And everything I keep within;
I've been locked up way too long
In this tower made of stone;
Let this ink bear the heartache,
For I still feel it in my bones –
A heaviness gradually increasing;
I am small and made of cracks;
Let this ink pour like lava
And dissolve my heart of wax

I'm sorry you have to put up with me;
So many hours I've ruined so far –
Stuck in my mind every single day
And it's tearing me apart, piece by piece;
Oh, how I ruin things, it's marvellous!
Withdrawing from life, my best trick,
While putting on a smile like cyanide –
There's nothing left on the horizon;
The sun has long set, but no one sees it:
I ruin things, I ruin things, I ruin *you*
That's what it's like if you're around me –
I am poison, I am toxic, I am horrendous;
Don't trust the ghost behind these eyes

Pour quicksilver from these eyes,
Hear the voices ringing in my ears;
I just want to fade into the ground,
Burning my way down towards hell –
I'll be the devil on your shoulder

These mind games I employ
To lure you in & take you down,
Distorting the bitter truth
And before you even know it –
You're stuck inside my trap,
In a net of confusion I spun,
Keeping you within reach;
No matter the distance you run –
You'll always end up here with me,
For I am a part of you, my dear;
Your thoughts & actions in my control:

I'm the voice inside your head

Images piercing skin,
Leaving a hole where
My soul anxiously hides;
Space & time dissolve,
As I prepare for this fight

My throat welcomes
The alluring dagger,
Severing the aorta
For a final breath
To lay memories to rest

Lightning in my brain,
Muscles twitching
For a split second –
I relive the past again –
My trauma time machine

My mind is a coffin
For all the secrets I'll never tell,
That even the pen cannot extract –
It's a mahogany casket,
For all my demons locked up airtight,
To breathe putrid air into their lungs –
The work of a monster I'm too familiar with,
Constantly screaming my name,
Until I surrender and fall apart;
I'm not alone in a forest screaming,
I'm in a room full of people –
A funeral home for the walking dead,
As I light a match & cremate what's left
Of my erratic soul feeling too much

A TANKA

Good morning, Darkness,
I see you're still here with me
Even though I tried

To rid myself of the pain,
I can't seem to let it go

These lips have lost their colour,
These eyes have lost their shine;
I know where it all went wrong,
But I was too frozen to move;
Change hurt more than trauma,
So I left it all as it was for you –
Putting on lipstick every day,
Wiping the tears off my cheeks;
You'd never know how I truly felt,
I've turned into a porcelain doll –
I exist, yes, but am I alive?

AN ACROSTIC

Moth-eaten madness is my
Old friend waving at me,
Meddling with my life –
Endlessly chewing sanity;
Not a moment goes by without
Thinking about the fallout

Unwanted memories linger on my brain
Like cobwebs dipped in bitter poison;
Macabre disguise of a tormented mind –
A labyrinth of paranoia and madness
Keeping me on my toes within these walls;
Crack my skull open to let some light in,
It's too cold and lonely here in the dark

A thousand stories woven
Into the fabric of the universe;
A spark to ignite potential,
Seemingly lost among neural pathways,
Resurfaces in a galaxy of promise –
If left malnourished, withers in silence,
As the cosmos in my skull deteriorates –
A black hole of unknown depth remains
And a thousand stories turn to ash

In my head it's already October,
But that's about as far as I
Would dare to think into the future,
For this autumn has me shifting shapes –
I'm accepting who I've become,
I'm no longer doing whatever it takes
To make every friend, every stranger,
Feel comfortable in the imaginary light;
I am the darkness, lest you forgot –
I no longer care if it hurts or not

macabre melancholy

FOURTH COURSE

Welcome to the Silva Obscura –
Where nothing is what it seems;
Deep into the woods, three ladies live
In a caliginous cottage, execrated;
Hidden away from sight of curious
Scaremongers & tattletales;
Inside their hut, they cook & brew
Various potions, long overdue
And you will *die* to try them –
If only they would make you
Stronger, wiser, more amiable

MACABRE MELANCHOLY

Scorching snowflakes on my skin –
The sensation strangely familiar
Where once embers gently fell,
Flowers bloomed and withered;
Wondrous weeds took their place
And thus a dark forest emerged;
In the land of the forever haunted,
I'm at home among the poison ivy –
During this seemingly endless winter,
I will continue to thrive

My worst nightmare
Is a sea full of spiders –
Moths & bats flying about;
I'm trying to run run   run,
But I am stuck here
On this skyscraper,
Watching the spiders
Crawl below like the tide;
I feel a sudden push and
I am falling, forever f a l l i n g
Until I hit the ground
And wake up – the moment,
When my nightmare ends and
Your worst nightmare begins

I'm the deadly nightshade
Growing inconspicuously
In the corners of your dreams;
Poisoning your memories –
Mildewed pollen resting
On your heavy eyelids;
I am in bloom, look at me!
How beautifully I deceive –
Drink from my violet cup
And rest assured, my love:
Dancing among the stars,
Your dreams will be immortal;
A mysterious vapour rises,
As you take your last breath

She is a woman with luminous hair –
Holding the thread of life in one hand
And the power of demise in the other;
Dahlias and dragonflies surround her,
As she summons the perpetual night;
Cruel clouds craving cotton candy carnage
And so let the morbid festivities begin!
Poisonous precipitation stains the pavement
Of ghost towns waiting for their turn,
For this night will be your very last!
So pray for her frostbitten, wispy fingers
To let you go gentle into that dark night

These words are not what you think –
Not the comfortable chair you're used to;
Pins & needles pierce the tattered fabric;
I'm lacking the clarity to embroider
These lacklustre lines with golden threads,
Creating something for you to admire;
No, these words are syllabic discomfort –
Tormenting the mind that feels,
Disturbing the mind that receives

Her heart stopped beating
One minute into the abyss;
Years of cruel malevolence
Had poisoned her mind
With bouts of hopelessness,
Had infected her heart
With suspicion & anxiety;
Pouring potential into pots
Cracked in a thunderstorm –
You won't forget her screams

I still remember everything –
It was a bright & beautiful day,
When her skeletal remains were found
On the bottom of the marshy lake;
Many months had passed ever since
Her worried mother saw her last;
"What happened to her?" — you may ask.
If only we could summon her soul
Among these ghosts that float about
A haunted place of immortal souls,
Resembling fog on a wintry night

Conjuring up feelings of indifference,
As they gradually take shape
In the form of carelessness & cruelty –
I cut the ties that bind me –
Sometimes I simply have to let go,
Even if it requires a numbness
For the souls left in the wake of destruction

MEDUSA'S SONG

Voices from the attic –
I hear them, or do I?
Speaking in tongues,
Am I under a spell?
I feel myself moving,
But as I look back –
I see myself aghast,
Standing in the hallway;
The attic comes closer
And I open the creaky door,
But before I even know it,
I'm turned to st---

SERENA MORRIGAN

A RONDEAU CINQUAIN

I've been searching near & far
For a heart as black as tar –
To match the colour of my veins,
Dipped in ink, held in chains,
To keep it in a jar

How beautifully hurt you are!
I promise this won't leave a scar;
A little cut to ease your pains

I've been searching near & far
For a heart as black as tar –
To match the colour of my veins

Together we will raise the bar,
Our broken souls as black as char –
They'll find a place where sorrow reigns,
Black clouds form, the dark remains;
Don't you find the view bizarre?

I've been searching near & far
For a heart as black as tar –
To match the colour of my veins,
Dipped in ink, held in chains,
To keep it in a jar

Waking from a nightmare, she lies
In a bed of thorns, picked by demise;
Another day, no glimmer in her sighs,
Thoughts forlorn, her heart unwise;
Tracing fingers, now dead and cold,
Rigid lungs ache for some air to hold:
This horrid dream roams uncontrolled,
As if it were meant to be left untold

THE OLD LADY IN THE MANSION

Down the street there's a majestic mansion –
Centuries old and neglected for decades;
No one lives there anymore, you'd think,
Except for the old lady in her bloodstained cloak
Who grins morbidly, making your blood run cold,
And hums a high-pitched melody, carried by the wind;
The thought of her leaves a shiver down your spine –
Who could be the lady of this haunted house?

It was ten years ago on All Hallow's Eve,
When the old lady in her light grey cloak
Moved in with all her cats and paradisiacal birds;
That evening, purple smoke rose from the chimney
And not a single living thing was seen
Leaving that haunted house ever again!
Yet she suddenly seemed twenty years younger –
What diabolical potion brewed in her cauldron that night?

Down the corridor adorned with photographs,
Blurry eyes pass me by as I set foot across the hall;
My peripheral vision – it deceives me, I fear,
For I see those faces moving, ever so slightly;
What are they trying to tell me with their rigid glances?
A pale brow turns to frowning, a warning, I assume –
Not to go any further near the deserted room;
Yet I continue my walk to obtain a precious painting
Of my great-grandmother's youthful days;
Out of sight for many generations, I've heard –
Whispers behind closed doors, are they true?
Curiosity gets the best of me and thus I proceed –
The opus under a veil of shadows therefore lies;
A thick carpet of dust remains untouched;
I take a deep breath & wave the grime goodbye –
Oh, my great-grandmother's beautiful eyes!
A curse watered down throughout the generations,
It spells my untimely end in bold letters:

MACABRE MELANCHOLY

Whoever dares to look into those eyes
May die an instant death and turn to dust
Resting calmly on the cursèd painting
Until the end of all days...

The fog rises ere the sun's first gleam,
As she slips through the graveyard's gates;
A black veil covering her ashen face
To attend tonight's dark ceremony;
The sacrifice of a bleeding thing
Under a sepulchral New Moon –
To fulfil the prophecy of the Three;
Calling her the Queen of the Dark,
She doesn't mind the price to pay –
This blood on her hands won't subside;
No, they will never be clean again
And thus she will remain, putrescent,
Sleepwalking on every Dark Moon
With a crimson veil covering her soul

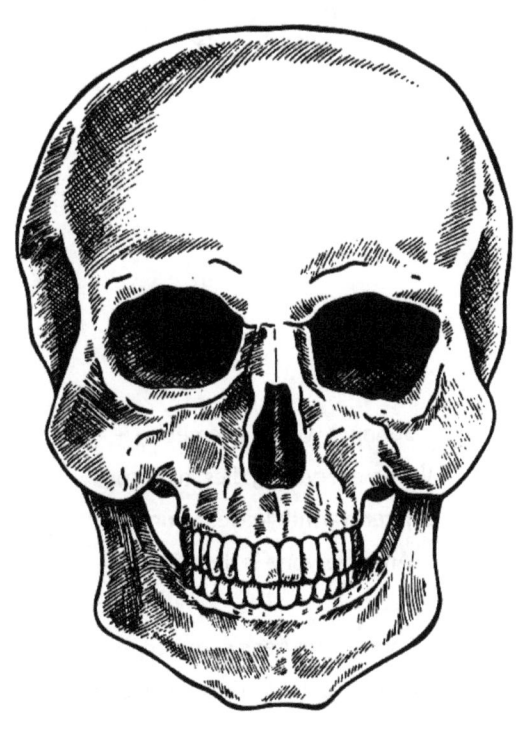

graveyard grimoire

FIFTH COURSE

Spring is winter's cemetery –
When everything dies in unison,
Winter warmth leaves your eyes,
And everyone is dead inside

Spring is winter's cemetery –
When the clouds grieve in unison,
Summer still so far away,
Watching it all fall apart again

GRAVEYARD GRIMOIRE

Cool summer nights at the cemetery,
Drinking gin like lemonade in the moonlight;
The cicadas, all the while, humming dirges
And us slowly, very s l o w l y
Decaying in the tall grass between tombstones

Willows weeping for times gone by,
Their whispers fill the misty air,
As life gradually comes to a halt;
They mourn the loss of their leaves
Uncertain if another spring may come,
The willows sing their sombre elegies,
In a language inaudible to you and I;
The branches swaying back and forth
To the wind's
                autumnal
                          symphony

All I can hear are the raindrops falling
And the weeping willows at the graveyard –
Their heavy branches caressing tombstones:
"I am one with death, one with grief," they sing;
Each leaf falling, an emerald tear for you,
Carried by the wind – fairies' breath –
To a secret hiding place only they know,
Leaving the trees' skeletons bare & frozen;
Let nature mourn another winter's arrival

DEDICATED TO
TED E. PENFOLD

I am old, I have seen many summers pass,
Have lent an ear to every lost soul I encountered,
Cradled every rootless vagrant needing shelter

I am old, my skin is wrinkled and scarred –
With every lover's name carved into the surface,
I have soothed every broken heart bleeding

I am old, and these hollow bones now echo
Whenever there's something stirring inside;
I don't have much time left on this earth

I am old, and my roots are brittle & loose,
And my leaves have long wilted in the autumn sun;
Next spring, I will nourish a new generation,
For I am old and I'm ready to go…

At nightfall when the fog is thick
And the birds retreat to their nests,
I take a walk across the graveyard,
To think about my past mistakes;
The cool & sombre air calms my mind –
It's been glowing hot like embers –
An infinitely burning fire in my head;
If I tell these resting souls my secrets,
To whom will they retell these tales?
I take a glance over my shoulder,
As ghosts play with my hair undone;
I'll never truly be alone here in the
Land of the Dead
I'll never truly feel at home in the
Land of the Living

Let the ghosts sing their elegies;
Let the ghosts sing of tragedies;
A song long forgotten – back alive,
When the ancestors assemble
And sing of love and loss and lore

"I've loved and lost –
Like so many before me,
Like so many coming after;
I've loved and lost,
And this pain keeps me alive"

Let the ghosts revive their memories;
Let the ghosts revive these bones;
As they continue singing elegies,
For the souls still trapped inside
A body wrecked by love and loss and lore

"I've loved and lost –
Like so many before me,
Like so many coming after;
I've loved and lost,
And this pain keeps me alive"

Let the ghosts sing...
Let the ghosts sing...
Let the ghosts sing...

I'm a ghost, a wandering spectre,
I carry nothing but my vapours;
The person I once was has died.
Thus I exist between the realms –
Never truly belonging anywhere;
I'm a ghost, a silent spectator,
Holding millions of thoughts –
Everything else just dissolves;
I am nothing but a molten creature,
Yet I move and I breathe, I'm alive!

I'm familiar with the
Darkness that surrounds me;
This pain is an old friend
Visiting my burial site –
Where I've sown sorrow,
Despair, and loneliness;
I watered it with blood
And tears – all I could give;
I patiently grew a rose bush,
Ready to prick me at any time;
Like Sleeping Beauty, I feel
This pull towards the thorn
And only a miracle
Can keep me away from home

The end is near –
I'm digging my own grave;
I don't feel safe here anymore;
Inch by inch, I shovel deeper
To lay my heavy bones to rest;
Peaceful sleep for the wicked –
I don't deserve anything else,
Still wondering who'll be left
When they finally discover
The monster underneath;
When everything, the flesh & bones,
Has rotten away eventually

I'll lie dormant forever,
Six feet deep in torpor;
Buried in layers of black sand,
Amidst the flowers & bones;
I'm an old unopened letter,
Taking my secrets to the grave;
Maybe one day I'll resurface
As a sprout in frozen soil,
But for now let me sleep –
I am tired, oh so tired

SERENA MORRIGAN

A TANKA

Empty graves echo
They had been buried alive
Or rather undead

For their hunger for brains grew
And now they're coming for you!

No matter what I do,
It's never going to be enough;
I am driftwood – long dead –
And your aquose words
Won't bring me back to life

AN OLD SONG

There's nothing left but
Perfidious parasites –
Nestled in my rootless heart
And thoughts begin to crawl
Through tortured skin;
The point of no return reached,
When my mind crosses a line

There's nothing left but
Persistent paranoia –
A devil resting on my shoulder
And life begins to show:
I'm fighting a losing battle;
These shadows will remain
And all my thoughts collide

Here in my world of fantasy
I am in charge, this is my design –
Ghosts of midnight eat away
At my fickle sanity, this is my decline

Flames nipping at this
Heart-shaped thing in my chest,
Singeing the edges of
Every syllable ever muttered;
Come & cut my origami heart
Into a thousand pieces
And scatter the remnants
On unholy grounds

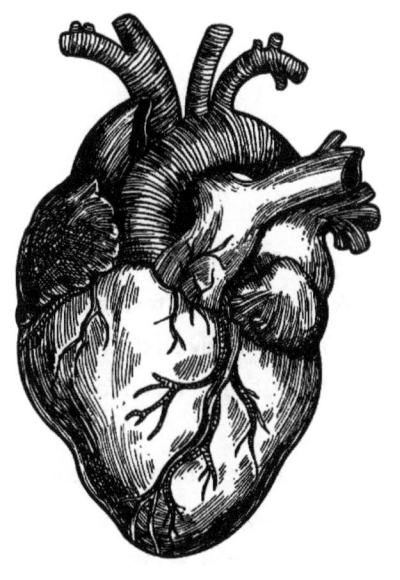

haunted hearts

SIXTH COURSE

Past the hallway
Where memory after memory
Lines up neatly on the walls,
You see, I never asked for this

When did these sweet mementos turn bitter?
I can barely look at them, eyes burning;
My heart breaking at every glance –
You wonder why I came here after all these years;
Well, I brought gasoline and a matchbox
And with the strike of a frail match,
I'll burn these reminders down to the ground
And breathe in the smoke of my past

I wanted to leave, but I stayed,
Watching the house burn down,
The structure disintegrate,
As my memories slowly drowned
In the flames, infernal cascade,
Spreading all across town

Sometimes I stop and realise –
Your whispers from beyond the grave
Suddenly ring true in my ruined ears:
"I am dead", you once said
And who'd have thought –
You really meant it

O sweet Nepenthe, make my heart forget
The pain inflicted by centuries of woe;
Let me drink this potion, so I can sleep,
Not wasting one more thought on the Wicked One

O sweet Nepenthe, though bitter on my tongue –
All the heartache dissolves when I'm with you,
For you place it in a vault far from view;
My agony waiting for me until morning comes

Get comfortable on this bed of nails,
For it is all you'll know from now on;
Let each point pierce the flawless flesh,
Until you feel a tingling on your skin;
The blood seeping into the wood –
Now you know how it feels to be
The outcast, the witch in barren fields

An old woman from Jakarta once stopped me,
Looked me in the eye, and spoke with a frown:

"Ada udang di balik batu"

'Twas a warning – how she knew, I'll never know,
For I had put all my trust in someone I once knew –
Believing they were a friend with good intentions,
When in fact they turned out to be a crustacean
With ulterior motives, hiding behind a boulder;
A precious translucent prawn, beautiful to look at,
Yet wretched in its ways, descaling my thoughts,
Until I was left scraped raw of all my hopes again

Let us be ghost friends forever,
We don't need to communicate;
I just want to know you're there,
How you took the other road –
And live another life without me;
Stay in the space between the planes,
Lead a life knowing/unknowing
That we're not friends anymore

You're living on
The dark side of the Moon –
A recluse; you've abandoned
The life you once knew,
Unable to notice
The silver from under my eyes –
A farewell for the forgotten

The world shook, silent quake;
Glass shattered, drums burst
In a moment of inadvertence;
Wails carried by the wind,
Tears flooding the tarmac,
Dark suppressing daylight –
How I remembered disaster,
As it hit the happiest heart;
Words lost their meaning
In a tsunami of sudden grief;
Sea foam soaked into
My ever-nocturnal heart

You don't know it yet,
But I am venomous,
Piercing your skin
With these white fangs;
I hide behind a smile
And an angelic voice,
Singing sweet lullabies,
Making you believe
That I am holy, but love,
This is your demise

You don't know the truth –
I'm a master manipulator,
I suck your blood and
You mistake it for a kiss;
The poison in your veins
Making you delusional;
I push you down to hell,
Leaving the illusion that
It's a heaven tailor-made
For you, only you

When the wind blows through the trees
And branches tap on your arching window,
Don't let your imagination mislead you –
For it is not as simple as you think, my dear,
When branches turn into greedy fingers
And the wind – a hungry werewolf's howl,
'Tis then you lie and shiver helplessly;
Sweet nightmares, love, don't sleep too tight

"I would eat his heart in the marketplace,"
She said as she crunched on one of his eyes;
He had annoyed her for quite some time –
With his awful stare and contemptuous words;
So one evening she went into his backyard
With a shotgun and a rifle, just to make sure
That his wicked heart would never beat again

This wicked heart, it taunts me;
Collecting memories on razor blades
Kept in this heart-shaped vessel –
I'll surely die of internal bleeding –
When time comes, I'll lose you too
And with vicious ardour I will try
To cut the image planted on my mind
Out of this useless rib cage

THE PHOENIX

Happiness has been reduced
To a gleaming ache in my heart;
Despair simmering to the surface,
Madness born out of ashes;
I'm burning, constantly burning,
Don't try to hold my hands –
Like embers illuminating the dark,
Scorching skin & flesh & bone;
A subtle glow, volcano virago

I feed my heart shrapnel for it to detonate –
An explosive mix of anger and bile,
Destroying everything in its wake;
One touch and you're dead, sudden blackness,
This shrapnel-filled heart's only purpose –
To bury the bodies in diseased debris

notes

NOTES ON SOME
OF THE POEMS

THE TIGHTROPE WALKER (p.19)

"funambulist" (noun)

a tightrope walker

CIRCUS MACABRE (p. 20)

"vaudeville" (noun)

A form of theatre popular from the 1880s through the 1920s, combining different kinds of short performances.

MARY'S REVENGE (p. 22)

Mary was an elephant who performed in a circus and killed one of her keepers in 1916. She was hanged afterwards.

AMUSEMENT PARK (p. 26)

Dreamland was an amusement park in New York City which opened in 1904, but a fire in 1911 destroyed most of the park.

THE DARKEST MIND (p. 28)

Dylan Thomas was a Welsh poet. This poem is inspired by one of his most popular works Do Not Go Gentle Into That Good Night (1947).

notes

CONTINUED

BELOVED (p. 48)

"acrostic" (noun)

A type of poetry in which the first letters in each line form a word
or phrase when read vertically, in this case the word "beloved".

THE SÉANCE (p. 50)

"séance" (noun)
A spiritualist meeting to communicate
with the spirits of the dead.

AT THE THEATRUM ANATOMICUM (p. 53)

"theatrum anatomicum" (noun)
A theatrum anatomicum, or anatomical theatre,
was a building or room used to teach
anatomy by dissecting animal and human bodies.

"memento mori" (noun)
An object or symbol used as a reminder of one's mortality,
literally meaning "be mindful of dying".

notes

CONTINUED

NO SUN TODAY (p.67)

"tanka" (noun)

A tanka is a form of Japanese five-line, unrhymed poem consisting of five, seven, five, seven, and seven syllables, or more.

SILVA OBSCURA (p. 76)

"silva" (noun)

The forest trees of a certain region.

"obscura" (adjective)

shadowy, indistinct

"caliginous" (adjective)

misty, obscure

"execrated" (adjective)

abhorred, hated, detested

notes

CONTINUED

BLACK HEART (p. 86)

"rondeau cinquain" (noun)

A form of mediæval French poetry consisting of 21 lines with the following rhyme scheme: AABBA, aab, AAB, aabba, AABBA.

NEPENTHE (p. 117)

"nepenthe" (noun)

A potion bringing relief from sorrow,
first mentioned in Homer's Odyssey.

ULTERIOR MOTIVES (p. 119)

"ada udang di balik batu" (proverb)

The Indonesian proverb (literally "there is a prawn behind the rock") means that there is a concealed ulterior motive.

THE BACKYARD (p. 125)

The phrase "I would eat his heart in the market place"
is taken from William Shakespeare's
Much Ado about Nothing, Act IV, Scene 1.

credits

THANK YOU TO THE EDITORS OF THE FOLLOWING JOURNALS

These are the volumes in which the poems "*At the Theatrum Anatomicum*" and "*Porcelain Doll*" first appeared:

"AT THE THEATRUM ANATOMICUM"

TRAIN RIVER POETRY

"PORCELAIN DOLL"

EVE POETRY MAGAZINE

acknowledgements

**A WARM THANK-YOU TO
EVERYBODY INVOLVED**

Thank you to Ralf for sticking with me through thick and thin, for your endless support and love. I wouldn't be here without you and I will be forever grateful for everything we've achieved in the last year alone.

Thank you to my daughter, my perfect little baby, for showing me what true happiness looks like. You are everything I've ever asked for. I hope I will instil in you my love for literature one day.

I would also like to thank Beth for being the awesome friend that she is and for making all my graphic design dreams come true. I've never met someone I vibe with like that before and I'm so grateful for our friendship! She also shares my weird taste in music to a T which is simply mind-blowing – and so much fun. I love this girl!

Then I'd also like to thank Brooke for doing me the honour of proofreading and editing this collection once again. I don't know what I'd do without your incredible feedback and expertise, it's simply amazing!

acknowledgements

CONTINUED

Furthermore, I'd love to thank Kim for all the dark inspiration you continue to spark in me. I thoroughly enjoy working with you on dark poetry collaborations and projects, and I can't wait to see what the future brings!

Lastly, I'd love to thank you, my reader, for your support. It means more to me than I can put into words. Honestly, thank you.

Serena

about the author
THE POET BEHIND THE BOOK

Serena Morrigan is a poet and mental health advocate. She started out on Instagram, posting poems in the hopes of finding kindred souls. Her work has since been published in several print and online publications, including Train River Poetry and Eve Poetry Magazine. Her first poetry collection *A Song for Every Scar* openly talks about mental illness and grief, and can be purchased online at all major retailers.

tara

INSTAGRAM:
@TARAGRIMRAVN

When offered the opportunity to review Serena Morrigan's new poetry collection, *Tea for the Wicked*, I have to say I was quite interested. The artwork alone was enough to tickle the sensibilities of the dark spiritual practitioner in me.

It's also no secret that, as a writer and editor, horror and dark fantasy are my absolute favorite genres. So, this work of pitch-dark poetry was right up my alley.

What I loved most about Morrigan's work in this book is that each poem within the six "courses" not only stands alone on its own merit but also plays a role within a larger story. This isn't simply a collection of random pieces; it's storytelling through verse. The imagery is haunting and beautiful, giving vivid life to each siren's song of shadow, as though reading a bit of Poe but crafted with far more modern sensibilities.

I absolutely enjoyed reading these well-woven, somber strains, and I highly recommend them to those who enjoy the sweet chill of the macabre.

Vera

INSTAGRAM:
@THE.VERSES.OF.VERA

In this book, Serena takes you to all the places your childhood (and present) nightmares consist of: Join her in the circus arena, juggling knives and fire, stroll through abandoned amusement parks and dimly-lit cobblestoned streets – maybe you'll find refuge in one of the candle-lit salons and participate in a séance, talking to the sad souls forgotten at the bottom of the swamp.

So grab yourself a cup of tea (for the wicked) and accompany Serena on her syllabic journey; let your soul tumble freely in between the tombstones, but don't expect to come home from this trip being the exact same person you were before.

kim

INSTAGRAM:
@WRITERPOETKIM

Serena Morrigan has created a deliciously dark poetry collection – *Tea for the Wicked* – that horror fans will love! Characters from classics like Frankenstein and Dracula are represented, as well as characters and situations of her own creation. Like her previous book, *A Song for Every Scar*, this text is visually stunning and very well-written. A tremendously fun read that I highly recommend!

aubree

INSTAGRAM:
@AUBREE.BARNUM

Tea for the Wicked is a unique compilation of the macabre and mystical. It's filled with everything I love — darkness, magic, and a sense of otherworldliness. Serena always has a way of working her magic with words and this collection is no exception.

Milton Keynes UK
Ingram Content Group UK Ltd.
UKHW021838041024
449101UK00013B/843